info buzz

Toys

Izzi Howell

W

FRANKLIN WATTS

LONDON · SYDNEY

Franklin Watts
First published in Great Britain in 2019 by The Watts Publishing Group
Copyright © The Watts Publishing Group, 2019

Produced for Franklin Watts by
White-Thomson Publishing Ltd
www.wtpub.co.uk

Credits
Series Editor: Izzi Howell
Series Designer: Rocket Design (East Anglia) Ltd
Designer: Clare Nicholas
Literacy Consultant: Kate Ruttle
Historical Consultant: Philip Parker

The publisher would like to thank the following for permission to reproduce their pictures: Alamy: KGPA Ltd cover, Beepstock 7r, ClassicStock 11r; Getty: Topical Press Agency title page, 4l and 10r, David Savill 5, tojanetoo 6l, studio22comua 7l, Brand X Pictures 8, FPG 10l, De Agostini Picture Library 12, Keystone-France\Gamma-Rapho 13t and 16r, H. Armstrong Roberts/ClassicStock 14, Dennis Hallinan 18, Picture Post 20, Dennis Hallinan 21t, Ingram Publishing 21b; Shutterstock: NY-P 4r, unclepepin 6c, Ruth Black 6r, enchanted_fairy 9t, Ivonne Wierink 9c, speedphotos 9b, Code2707 11l, Veja 13b, goodmoments 15, ANGHI 16l, Antonio Petrone 17, robtek 19t, ThomasDeco 19b.

Printed in China

Franklin Watts
An imprint of
Hachette Children's Group
Part of The Watts Publishing Group
Carmelite House
50 Victoria Embankment
London EC4Y 0DZ

An Hachette UK Company
www.hachette.co.uk
www.franklinwatts.co.uk

MIX
Paper from
responsible sources
FSC® C104740

All words in **bold** appear in the glossary on page 23.

Contents

Then and now

Children have always played with toys. Some toys from the past aren't played with today.

These children are playing with hoops. They hit the hoop with a stick to make it roll along. ▼

1920s

Victorian

This toy was **popular** in **Victorian** times. Children tried to catch the ball in the cup. ▶

Children look at wooden toys in a toy shop.

1930s

LORRY 46

RICKSHAW 1

In the past, toys were made from wood, metal or fabric. Today, most toys are made from plastic or fabric.

Which toys on these pages are not played with today?

Dolls

Dolls were made from different **materials** in the past. In Victorian times, they were made from **china**. In the 1920s and 1930s, dolls started to be made from plastic.

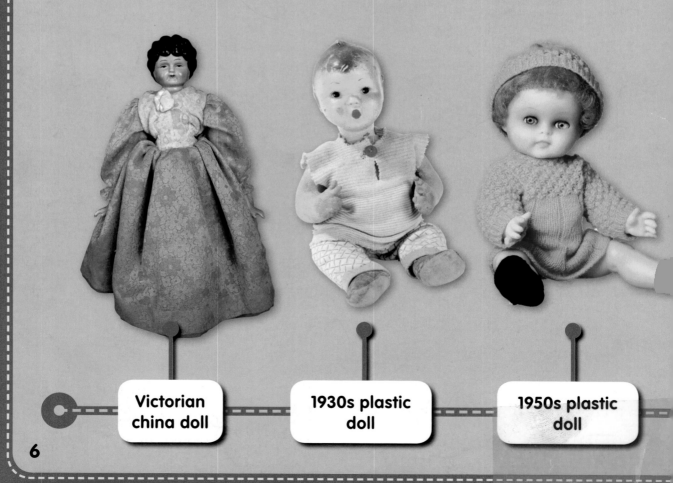

Victorian china doll

1930s plastic doll

1950s plastic doll

The clothes that dolls wear have changed over time. Dolls often wear clothes that are **in fashion** at the time they are made.

Can you spot three differences between the oldest and newest dolls on these pages?

1980s plastic dolls

modern plastic doll

7

Soft toys

Some of the first soft toys were teddy bears. They were made about 120 years ago.

◀ Teddy bears were made from furry fabric.

1910s

Today, there are many types of soft toys. They look like different animals, people or objects.

These modern soft toys are in the shape of a fox, a rooster and a car.

What soft toys do you have?

9

Trains, boats and cars

In the past, children played with toy trains and boats. At first, they were simple toys. Later, **electric** toys that could move by themselves were sold.

These children are sailing a wooden boat on a lake. ▶

1910s

1950s

◀ This electric train moves around a track.

Children started playing with toy cars in the 1900s. This is the same time that people started to drive real cars.

Some toy cars were small.

1900s

Other toy cars were big enough to ride in. ▶

1930s

Board games

Many people played board games 100 years ago. Some of these board games aren't sold today.

In this cycling board game, players tried to get their cyclist to the end of the race in the centre of the board.

Some board games from the past are still played today.

1930s

today

▲ These friends are playing chess together. Chess is still a popular game.

The game Monopoly was first sold in 1935. It is still popular today. ▶

Puzzles

Jigsaw puzzles have been popular since before Victorian times. Then, they were made of wood. Today, they are usually made of cardboard.

▼ This family is working on a jigsaw puzzle together.

1970s

1980s

What puzzles do you have?

In some puzzles, you have to solve a problem.

▲

To solve a Rubik's Cube puzzle, you have to move the squares to make all the squares on each side the same colour.

15

Building blocks

Children have always liked to build things. They built with wooden blocks in Victorian times. Later, children built using sets of metal pieces.

This boy has built a ferris wheel from a Meccano metal building set. ▼

1950s

Meccano metal building pieces ▼

In the 1940s, plastic building sets were sold. Children could **design** and build their own building. They could also follow instructions to build a special **model**.

▲ Lego building blocks are still popular today.

What's the best Lego model you have built? What did it look like?

Computer games

The first computer games were made in the 1970s and 1980s. Only a few people had computer games at home.

1980s

◀ These children are playing a computer game together.

What kinds of computer games do you play? What do you play them on?

In the 1980s, children started to play with **handheld** computer games. They could be taken outside of the house.

1990s

Lots of different games could be played on a Game Boy **console**. ▶

Today

▲
People often play games on their mobile phones today.

19

Playing outdoors

In the past, children played outdoors with balls, skipping ropes and hoops.

You can skip with friends or on your own.
▼

1940s

Later, children played with new outdoor toys, such as pogo sticks and space hoppers.

1960s

These boys are jumping high on pogo sticks. ▶

Children have played with space hoppers since the end of the 1960s. ▼

today

Which is your favourite toy in this book?

21

Quiz

Test how much you remember.

Check your answers on page 24.

1 Which materials were toys often made from in the past?

2 When did dolls start to be made from plastic?

3 How do you solve a Rubik's Cube?

4 What is Meccano made of?

5 When were the first computer games made?

6 Where should you play with a pogo stick?

Glossary

china – a hard substance that plates and teacups are made from

console – an object with which you can play computer games

design – to draw and plan something before making it

electric – powered by electricity

handheld – describes something that is small enough to be held in a hand

in fashion – describes clothes that are popular at one time

material – something from which other objects can be made, such as wood

model – a small version of an object or place

modern – describes something from today

popular – liked by many people

Victorian – from the years 1837 to 1901 in Britain, when Queen Victoria ruled the country

Index

Answers:

1: Metal, wood and fabric; 2: The 1920s and 1930s; 3: Move the squares to make each side a different colour; 4: Metal; 5: 1970s and 1980s; Outdoors

Teaching notes:

Children who are reading Book band Purple or above should be able to enjoy this book with some independence. Other children will need more support.

Before you share the book:

• Ask children what they think a toy is? Between them, can you agree on a definition?

• Let children think about their favourite toy and tell a response partner what it is.

While you share the book:

• Help children to read some of the more unfamiliar words.

• Talk about the questions. Encourage children to make links between their own experiences and the information in the book.

• Discuss the pictures, talking about which toys are familiar and which are not.

After you have shared the book:

• Let children identify toys in catalogues, cut out pictures and sort them according to different criteria (e.g. what they are made from).

• Let children compile a questionnaire to ask their parents/grandparents about toys they played with. Ask children to find pictures of the toys.

• If you have access to a museum with toys from the past, take the children for a visit. Otherwise, show them images from a online museum of toys or of childhood (e.g. The V&A Museum of Childhood at http://www.revolvingpicture.com/virtual-tours/moc/).

• Work through the free activity sheets at www.hachetteschools.co.uk

FRANKLIN WATTS